HOW TO BE A
Better
Footballer

HOW TO BE A
Better
Footballer

ANDREW HENDERSON

Michael O'Mara Books Limited

Contents

Introduction

I grew up in Cornwall and was a sporty kid – I was
always trying different activities and games. I played
a lot of table tennis, racket sports, I did cross-country
and long jump and I loved being active. Football was
my first love, though. It was everything to me.

**❛As soon as I could walk,
I was playing football.
It was my first passion.❜**

I played football at every opportunity and my
love for the game didn't dwindle as I grew older.
When I was a teenager, I started becoming
frustrated – not with the game – but by the
lack of opportunity to play.

'You can't stop and quit when something bad happens. You have to keep going and find a way to make it work.'

The club I played for was managed by another player's dad and that player played at the same position as me. This meant, although I was one of the club's top goalscorers, I was sitting on the bench a lot of time.

It was my cousin who suggested that I should play rugby with him at the weekend instead. And it was an easy decision to make for a very sporty teenager – sit on a bench and watch football or play a different sport? Of course I wanted to play! It was a perfect solution and as soon as I tried rugby, I fell in love with it. This is great, I thought, things happen for a reason. Perhaps playing rugby is what I am meant to be doing.

From a young age I knew I wanted to play sport for my country. I was so focused on that, it was a passion, a motivation and I knew I wanted to be a World Champion – but in which sport? Should I choose football? Rugby? Or was there another sport out there that I hadn't tried in which I might excel? I didn't want to make a bad decision because if I chose the wrong sport, I wouldn't achieve anything …

Fate and freestyle

I was sixteen years old when my life changed forever.

I had been selected to play rugby for my new club in a cup match against Truro, a club I had previously played with for a few years. The whistle went for the start of the match and straight away I was involved in the first play of the game. I caught the ball and started to run up the sideline and then decided to move direction and took an inside step, but as I put my foot down, it got stuck in the ground. The pitch was waterlogged and my body twisted while my foot stayed where it was and I came crashing to the ground. I broke my left leg in five places, through my tibia and fibula, and I dislocated my ankle.

'In case you think I was just at home having fun learning new skills, I didn't get out of schoolwork!'

It was such a bad injury that I had to have several operations on my broken leg, where surgeons inserted a metal plate and nine screws. But the worst was yet to come. The doctors told me I might never be able to walk again, let alone play sport – and I was shocked. As I said earlier, sport was everything to me. It was a massive part of who I was and to hear that news was devastating. My dreams were shattered.

Getting focused

Recovering fully from my injury took a long time – it was a year and a half until I was fully fit again – but two important things happened in that time. Firstly, I did walk again, and secondly, I found a love for a sport that up until that moment, I hadn't even been aware of.

When my leg was in a plaster cast I saw a video of a guy doing some tricks with a football that looked impossible. Before my injury, I had done a bit of kicking the ball up and trying to control it, but these skills were incredible. I realized that I could learn some of them, even with my injuries, and at that moment I had something to aim for. I had a focus again. I learned how to balance a ball on the top of my head, on the side of my head, even on my shin when I still had my leg cast on. It really helped my recovery because it gave me something to concentrate on and become motivated about. Learning these skills helped in my recovery process and stopped my rehabilitation from being a very boring and frustrating time.

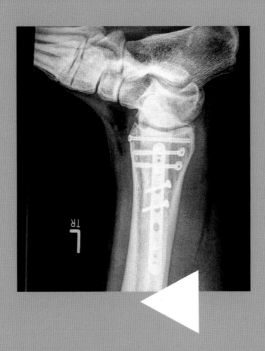

Freestyle Championships

I sat my exams and went on to college and made
a good recovery. It was about a year and a half until
I was fully recovered and during that time I was
getting really involved in freestyle football, training
when I could, while studying for my A Levels.

I found out that there was a National Championships in
freestyle football, an event that Red Bull was hosting,
and so I decided to go for it. What did I have to lose?
I signed up for the competition and was ecstatic to
make it through the first round. I was then invited to

travel to Bristol, where I would be taking part in the qualifiers for the Championships – and I won. So now I was through to the National Finals in London and I ended up winning that! I was the youngest National Champion at the time, at seventeen years old.

Think Big

A manager approached me at the event and told me something I didn't think was possible: that I could make freestyle football my full-time job. I had no idea I might be able to earn a living from this. It was crazy! He came down to Cornwall to persuade my parents that this was a real opportunity for me, and although they weren't easily convinced, I knew I wanted to pursue this new career. I had applied and been accepted for a university course but I knew that I had to focus on my dream – to be a World Champion in this sport and push myself as hard as I could to achieve it. So, I withdrew my university application the day before I was due to leave and I have never looked back. I won my first Freestyle World Championships the following year, in September 2011, and I have since become a five-time World Champion and eight-time UK National Champion. I know all my hard work, commitment, hours upon hours of training and focus was worth it and it's a real privilege to be labelled 'the greatest of all time' in this sport.

'I had no idea I might be able to earn a living from this. It was crazy!'

INSPIRATION FROM MY DAD

My dad competed at a high level in Judo. He was a British University champion and he trained with the Great Britain Olympic squad. Growing up and seeing that level of dedication and passion for a sport was inspiring. I knew I wanted to be the same, I wanted that feeling in a sport that I loved. It was something Dad completely understood, and he taught me to never give up. 'If you believe in something, keep working and working at it,' he would say. 'You will get there.'

What is Freestyle Football?

Freestyle football is a sport in its own right but it is about being creative and using your individuality. It probably falls between an art form and a sport.

You express yourself with a football. You perform a combination of fluid movement and creativity with a ball that is under complete control.

The origins of freestyle football aren't certain, some of the earliest evidence of freestyle skills were performed by a German guy called Francis Brunn, who was a circus performer. He joined a travelling show in 1939 and performed across Europe and America. He was best known for performing routines with a single ball that would look simple but required a lot of control and skill.

Freestyle football as we know it today took a lot of inspiration from Diego Maradona. He was a legend, he was a pioneer and he inspired me hugely. I would watch videos of him every morning before I started practicing. He brought some of these fundamental freestyle moves onto a worldwide stage and began the association of the art form with the sport of football.

CHINLONE

The national sport in Burma is called Chinlone in which they do something very similar to freestyle football. It's a non-competitive sport, where a team of six people – men, women and children – pass the ball around to each other, without using their hands, while walking in a circle. The idea is to pass the ball around the circle as creatively as possible, without it hitting the ground. It's not about winning, it's about expression and creating new movements and skills.

Practice Zone

Finding your practice zone

The good thing about freestyle football is that you can practise most of the skills anywhere, at any time – and you don't have to be using a football! Whether you're working on your Sits Juggling (see page 62) while watching the TV, kick-ups (see page 50) with an orange, or using a set area of your garden to try to bring your skills under control, it's all about using your environment.

Limiting your practice space

CONES

This is a practice drill to improve your ball control. It will really help you to concentrate on the skill you are practising and is particularly good for trying to beat your kick-up target. When you get used to working within a small area, you instantly feel more precise and focused.

Create a circle using cones or anything else you can use that marks out an area on the ground. The key is to practise the skills you are working on inside the circle of cones.

If you are finding the skill too easy, make the circle size smaller, if it seems too tricky, make the size of the circle slightly bigger and keep within the cones.

Set yourself some goals: how tight can you make your circle? How controlled can you be? What is your target today? It's always good to have an aim and set yourself a challenge.

Using objects other than a football

Playing with smaller objects will make you focus on the skill more as these items are harder to handle. Smaller, rounder objects are good because there is less surface area with which to make a connection with the ball and keep it going in the right direction. To control it means you really have to concentrate.

▷ Use oranges, mini footballs, tennis balls, rolled-up socks – whatever you have available!

▷ There is less room for error with a smaller object so it will really help to improve your control.

When you then go back to a normal-sized football, the skills will seem a lot easier. Any variation on training, whether it be with a different object or in a smaller/larger area, will help with your balance, your first touch and overall ball control, which are all essential for freestyle football.

Training with different objects improves your reactions as well. I sometimes train with a rugby ball because it reacts differently when it bounces on the ground. It keeps me light on my feet as I have to be focused and quick to follow it.

Wall Control

Wall control is all about working on controlling the ball and your balance. It will help with reactions, first touch and accuracy and you don't need a training partner for this skill, just a wall!

This is a great warm-up skill, that will get you focused, reactive and improve your ball control.

1 Stand about 5ft away from the wall and drop the ball in front of you. Wait for it to bounce and then using the side of your foot, connect with the ball and aim for the wall.

2 You don't have to have a specific circle or spot drawn on the wall for this. Find a target in your mind you want to aim for and guide the ball with your feet towards the target.

3 You want to hit this at medium power - too hard and the ball will come back too fast and you will lose control. This is all about building a rhythm and control.

4 Good balance and good posture is important. Keep your hands out for balance and when the ball comes back to you, control it and cushion it with the side of your foot and then return it to the wall.

5 Try to practice with both feet so you have equal control whichever foot you use. As you begin to feel more confident, increase or decrease your distance from the wall, but keep the power with which you kick the ball the same. The further you move away from the wall you will find you have more time to react, the closer you are to the wall your reactions will need to be quicker.

Headers

Anyone can head a ball, but controlling a header is something that requires practice. The key advice to remember is this: Never. Take. Your. Eyes. Off. The. Ball!

1 Your starting position for this skill should be standing with your feet shoulder-width apart.

2 With the ball in both hands, throw it up in the air about 6 inches above your head and as it comes down, bend your knees into a slight squat position. Just when the ball hits your head, spring your body back up with the ball.

3 The connection point for the ball is right in the middle of your forehead and it helps to bring your arms out by your side for balance.

4 Stay light on your feet so that if the ball moves to one side you can follow it and remain in control, always getting back under the ball into your starting position.

5 The key to this skill is to build up a steady rhythm of headers, keeping your eye on the ball and making sure each header is as controlled as it can be.

This is a great confidence builder and it's fun to set yourself records to beat each time you do it. Once you have mastered heading the ball at a certain height, experiment going higher and higher. It's harder to control the more height you have, but if you can control the connection when it comes down you'll feel amazing!

Motivation, Motivation, Motivation

Once you spend time mastering the basics, you will always have that. It's like learning to ride a bike, you won't ever forget.

The great thing about freestyle football is that you are learning something every time you try a new trick – you are learning how to react to a ball, how to control it and, of course, the new skill itself. The more you learn, the more fun it is. It is hard at the beginning, as you don't wake up being a Freestyle Football World Champion.

You have to give yourself time to develop and practice. And once you have the basics it just gets more and more fun. It's like learning to ride a bike: it's frustrating at first, but once you've got it – you've got it! You don't even have to think about what you're doing, you just do it. That is the same with a lot of these tricks.

Enjoy yourself, this is fun!

> **'Not giving up is a skill that not many people will ever master.'**

Absolutely anyone can learn these skills, there is no excuse! All you need is dedication, focus and some self-belief. Having confidence and a 'never give up' attitude is the only requirement.

What keeps me motivated

I have built up a great career as a freestyle footballer. It's what I'm known for and it's my job but I always want to try new things, which is why I am also focusing on making it as a professional mixed martial artist. I'm going into a sport that is dangerous and new and there will be a lot of criticism and risk involved. But you should never regret not going for things just because you might be a bit scared or intimidated. I won't let being afraid or worried that things won't work out stop me from trying to be a professional MMA. And I will always keep doing my freestyle, of course, but I don't want you to ever be afraid of trying something new.

TOP TIP: Music

Music is a big motivator for me and when I am getting frustrated with how my training is going, I will often put on some tunes to keep me motivated.

Setbacks, shoulders and success

Did I tell you after I had broken my leg during my rugby game, I also broke my shoulder and arm about ten months later? I've got a metal plate and nine screws in there; you would think after damaging my leg so badly I would be more careful! Getting injured has, however, grounded me in a sense: I realized how reckless and crazy I was! I am not indestructible, I appreciate that now and even though I have had lots of injuries and setbacks, I am still going strong. Sometimes you have to get up and start again, even if you have suffered an injury or setback. But only you can have that motivation; no one can do it for you except you!

'You might not think you are making progress and have days when you can't seem to master the skills, but even slow progress is better than nothing! Stay positive and stay focused.'

Motivation and nutrition

To keep yourself mentally focused and motivated
you need to make sure you are putting the
right things into your body so that it can work
and do exactly what you want it to do.

Here are my Top 5 Tips to staying healthy:

Make sure you drink plenty of water

Water will keep your brain and your body hydrated – it
is essential! I always have a water bottle with me during
training and I make sure I finish it every session.

Don't train on an empty stomach

Food is the fuel for your body. You wouldn't play with a
football that had no air in it, would you? Of course not,
the football wouldn't bounce like it should. Make sure you
fill up with enough food to keep your energy levels high.

Eat plenty of fruit and vegetables

This is something you have heard before, right? Of course it is, and for good reason! I love fresh fruit and have a plate full of vegetables most mealtimes.

Cut down on sugar and fizzy drinks

Again, this isn't rocket science. Think about your flat football again: if you fill it up with sugar instead of what it needs (air!), what will happen? It will be heavy and sluggish and you will get tired very easily. It's the same thing when we eat too many sugary sweets, treats and fizzy drinks. We need to give our body the good, healthy stuff for it to work.

Give yourself occasional treats

This isn't to say you can't treat yourself! I make sure that I eat healthily but I know that the occasional chocolate bar or sweet is OK too. And you will enjoy it so much more when you know you've earned it.

Andy Murray

I was contacted by Amazon to make a video with tennis star and former Wimbledon champion Andy Murray. I love tennis and I often use tennis balls to perfect my skills, so this was great fun.

I helped him choreograph some skills he had been asked to perform with a tennis ball and I have to say, he was pretty impressive with his freestyle tricks! We filmed in his living room, doing some kick-ups and he told me how he also varies his training methods to improve all aspects of his tennis. He said he had even been learning break-dancing to improve his flexibility on the tennis court! He was such a lovely guy with a great sense of humour and I wouldn't be surprised if he pulled out some top freestyle moves on the court one day.

It's really interesting to hear how top athletes and sports stars train and what they do to keep mentally focused. Never be afraid to try different methods of learning and training. What have you got to lose?

Hot Steppers

This football freestyle skill is about bouncing the ball underneath the soles of your feet and building up a rhythm, a bit like a march or a jog.

1 Start by letting the ball drop down in front of you and, standing on one leg, bouncing it down with the sole of your foot with the other leg.

2 Keep bouncing it up and down in a controlled way, using the sole of your foot.

40

3 Then switch to bouncing and controlling it with your weaker leg. So stand on your stronger leg and see if you can get a rhythm using your weaker leg.

4 When you are feeling confident on both legs, alternate them and bounce the ball between both in a controlled rhythm.

5 Putting your hands out to the side helps. The pace should be as if you are jogging on the spot: every time you bring one leg up, the other leg goes down. The more power you put into pushing the ball down onto the ground, the quicker the ball is going to pop right back up at you, which makes it harder to control. Find a good balance between the speed you move at and the power you use.

Foot Stall

1.0 RATING ★☆☆☆☆ **SKILL LEVEL**

See how high you can bring your leg up while keeping the ball in a foot stall position. You'll need to keep your arms out for balance!

This is all about balancing the ball on the top of your foot, effectively trapping it between your foot and shin.

1 Start by standing with one foot slightly raised in front of the other and move your toes on that foot so they are pointing straight up.

2 Now place the ball in the angled space you have made with your foot and see how long you can trap it against your shin, keeping your arms out for balance.

3 Once you can balance that for a while, try to catch the ball in a foot stall position from juggles, making sure you bring your leg slightly higher off the ground when you do this, to cushion the ball as it comes down.

Jester

This is an easy freestyle trick to learn and looks pretty impressive once you've put all the steps together. You can use it in a football game where you kick the ball up over a player to beat your opponent. It shouldn't take too long to master either. Just put the steps together and keep on practising.

1 Start with the ball in your hands and drop it right in front of you.

2 Bring your strong leg over the front of the ball, step over it as the ball is bouncing on the ground.

3 Turn your other leg and hit the ball with the side of the foot, almost a half-volley touch with the ball just as it's bouncing back up.

4 Control it with your stronger foot on the upward bounce.

5 Once you get more confident, you can do this trick from kick-ups, but to begin with it's easier to start doing it by dropping, not bouncing, the ball with your hands.

Q&A
All About Me

Describe yourself in three words

Obsessed, energetic, focused.

What is your favourite food/meal?

I love Asian culture, so Thai food is a favourite of mine. I love that there are lots of different options and it's quite healthy. I enjoy cooking Thai meals and using fresh ingredients.

What was your favourite subject at school?

Geography. I was and still am very interested in finding out about different countries and other cultures. I always wanted to travel when I was a kid. I grew up in Cornwall, in the south-west corner of England, and I wanted to explore more of the world. It was a dream of mine to move to London.

Cats or dogs?

Dogs. My father has two Border collies. I love them!

What's the naughtiest thing you have ever done?

I once set off the fire alarm when I was at school. I was standing in the lunch queue and it was taking so long and me and my two friends were so bored! One of my friends put his hand a few inches away from the fire alarm, my other friend put his hand right over it and then I thought I would lightly touch it – and it went off. The Headteacher knew it was me because everyone else ran out to the tennis courts and lined up, while I went into the canteen for lunch because I knew there wasn't a real fire – and I was hungry.

What is your favourite TV show?

I love shows about nature, I love finding out about our planet. I love animals and learning new things.

What is your most annoying habit?

Clicking my neck. I do it with my jaw as well. It's not the nicest thing to watch. I think when I am doing a lot of tricks with my head and neck, and moving them really fast, they can get a bit stiff when I take a break and then I have to crank them a little.

Where is your favourite place to go on holiday?

I love Brazil. I went there for the 2014 World Cup and that was just an amazing experience. I hiked around the mountains and chilled on the beach, swam in the sea, ate lots of nice food and, of course, experienced the football culture too. I love South Africa and Oman. I have been to over fifty countries, so it's very hard to choose.

What is your favourite joke?

Which soccer team has nailed their formation?
The Hammers!

Which song always makes you smile?

There aren't any specific ones, any upbeat, fun songs will do. Sometimes I purposely train without music for the first hour or two, and then if I find myself getting frustrated, I put on some music. It keeps me focused for a little bit longer.

Kick-ups

1.0 RATING ★★★★★

SKILL LEVEL

This is one of the fundamental skills, the key to freestyle. It's like walking in the freestyle world. It forms the basis of all the other tricks.

It's very important to stay nice and relaxed. If your body is too tense and too stiff you won't be able to control the ball. It's all about feeding off the ball and controlling it.

1 Let the ball bounce in front of you and then kick it up with your strong foot to knee height.

2 You need to kick the ball on the part of your foot that is just in front of your laces.

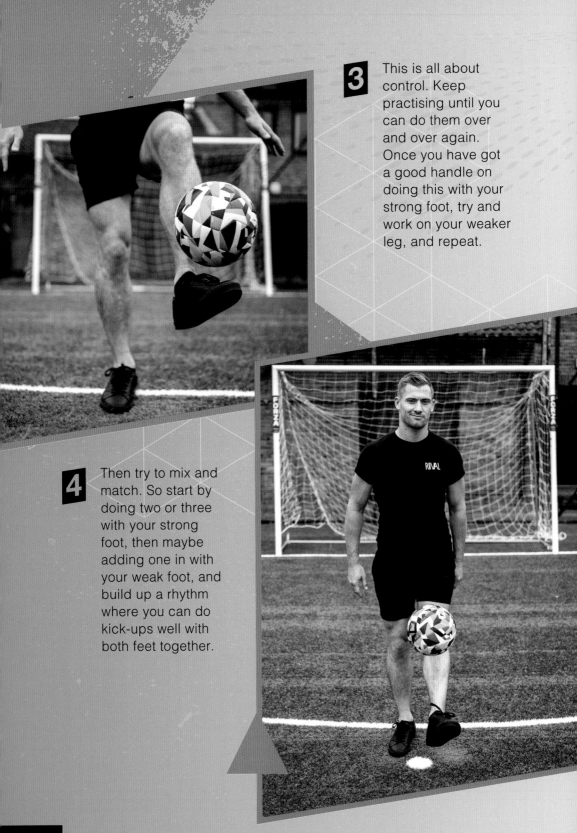

3 This is all about control. Keep practising until you can do them over and over again. Once you have got a good handle on doing this with your strong foot, try and work on your weaker leg, and repeat.

4 Then try to mix and match. So start by doing two or three with your strong foot, then maybe adding one in with your weak foot, and build up a rhythm where you can do kick-ups well with both feet together.

Knee Juggles

1.0 RATING

★ ☆ ☆ ☆ ☆

SKILL LEVEL

Being able to control the ball with your knees is another fundamental element of freestyle. It is similar to kick-ups in the rhythm and difficulty but the difference is that you use your knees to control the ball.

1 Stay nice and loose and relaxed. Try to drive your knee up and maintain balance when you are standing on one foot. To help with control and balance, bring your arms out wide.

2 Aim to juggle the ball just above your kneecap and every time you make a connection with the ball, you want to be moving your leg in and out of that 90-degree angle when you lift your leg.

3 Don't let the ball go above head height initially. You are controlling the height and power you put in, so maintain that height.

4 It's important to work off both knees, so practise your weak side as well as your stronger side.

5 Test yourself and see how many you can do!

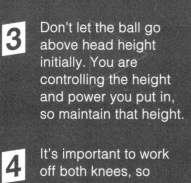

Rocket Launcher

1.0 RATING

⭐ ☆ ☆ ☆ ☆

SKILL LEVEL

This is a good move to get you into kick-ups, but if you haven't built up enough confidence with your kick-ups yet, simply practice catching the ball with your hands at the end.

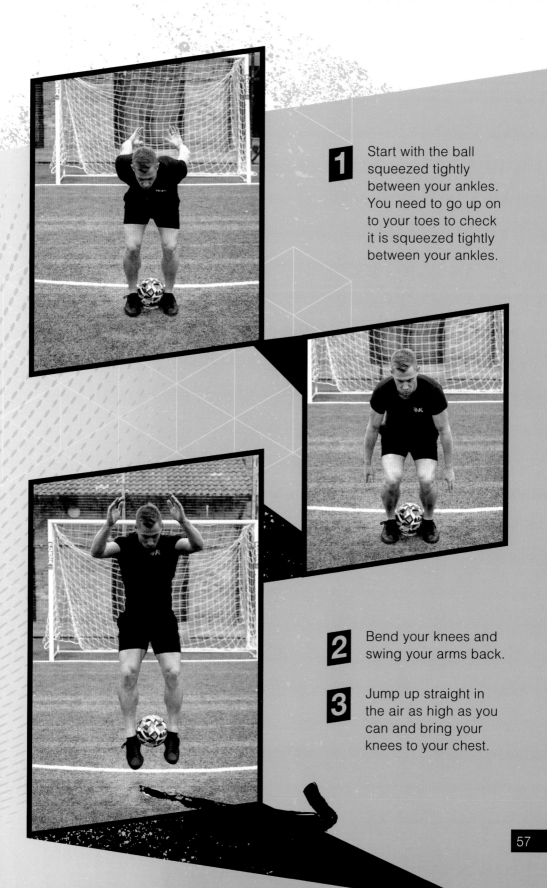

1 Start with the ball squeezed tightly between your ankles. You need to go up on to your toes to check it is squeezed tightly between your ankles.

2 Bend your knees and swing your arms back.

3 Jump up straight in the air as high as you can and bring your knees to your chest.

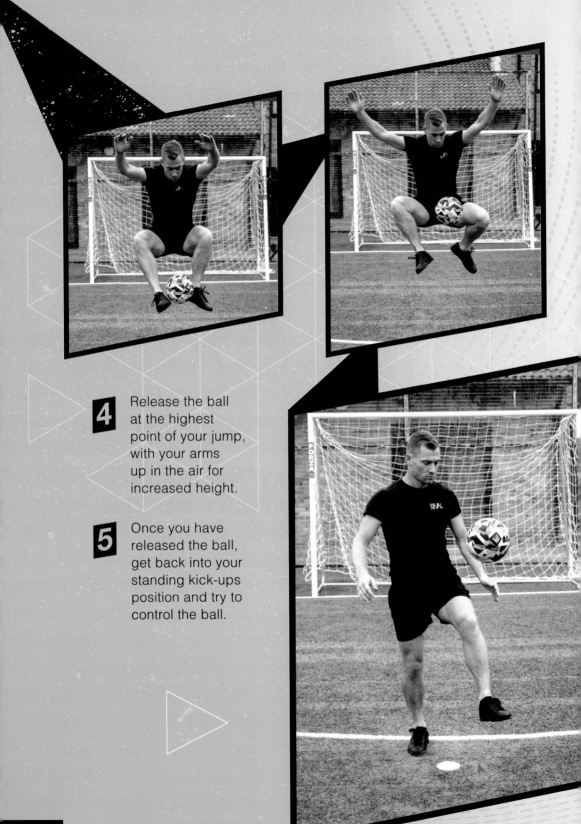

4 Release the ball at the highest point of your jump, with your arms up in the air for increased height.

5 Once you have released the ball, get back into your standing kick-ups position and try to control the ball.

Harry Kane

> **'It's good to take advice from other people but in the end you have to make your own decisions.'**

I met Harry Kane when I was doing a campaign in the build-up to the 2018 World Cup in Russia. We talked about the preparation for the tournament and what he thought of England's chances. He was really interested in freestyle football, so I showed him lots of tricks and skills.

Harry is a very steady footballer. When he plays it doesn't involve a lot of flair or a great many tricks, but he was fascinated with what I showed him and the different ways you can control a football. He wasn't allowed to have a go at the tricks as his management didn't want him to risk injury just before the World Cup – although I think he wanted to try! He was a very motivational person and a really hardworking, humble guy.

'LIONS DON'T LOSE SLEEP OVER THE OPINIONS OF SHEEP.'

Harry told me he works by this quote and it really stuck in my mind. In any sport you will find people who will give their opinions and tell you what they think, regardless of their own capabilities.

Harry endured lots of people giving their opinions on the England team and him as a captain, but they weren't training like him, they hadn't gone through what he had to become England Captain. Of course, it's good to take onboard advice from other people but in the end, it's down to you. You must have confidence in everything you do.

Sits Juggling

2.0 RATING ★★☆☆☆ *SKILL LEVEL*

Sit-down juggling is basically doing kick-ups while sitting on the ground. It's important to have your hands flat on the floor to ensure a good posture and keep your body well balanced.

1 Point your toes forwards and start with the ball between your legs.

2 You are aiming to hit the ball on the area of your foot where your laces are.

3 You don't need to kick it up very high, around about knee height is fine. Again, the higher you kick the ball, the harder it is to control.

180° Flick

1.0
RATING

★ ★ ★ ★ ★

SKILL LEVEL

This is a good skill to use on the football pitch as a way of helping you change direction and move past an opponent.

1 Start with the ball squeezed between your ankles, with your feet parallel.

2 Twist your torso around, so you are now looking slightly behind you.

3 And then, with your strong leg, begin to roll the ball up the back of the calf of your standing leg. Make sure you keep the ball trapped between the foot of your strong leg and the calf of your standing leg.

4 As you do this you need to rotate your body 180-degrees in a clockwise direction if you are right-footed and anti-clockwise if you are left-footed. Keep your arms out for balance.

5 Finish the rotation and control the ball back into foot juggles. You need to put all this together in quick succession to complete the move.

Knee Akka

This is a street football move in which you use your knee to flick the ball over your opponent. It's a certain skill that can be used in freestyle football or street football.

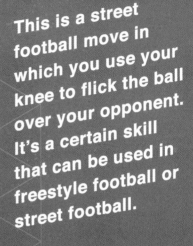

1 You flick the ball off the ground by rolling it back with the sole of your foot.

This is one of my favourite skills. It sounds complicated but once you have put all the parts together it's a really effective, useful trick.

2 With the ball rolled up onto your foot, flick it up into the air.

3 Move the ball out to the side with your knee.

4 And then you flick it with your outstretched foot to the side and up in the air.

5 The ball has now moved past your opponent, overhead, and you can run around to it and bring it back under control.

Rainbow Flick

2.0 RATING ★★☆☆☆ **SKILL LEVEL**

The Rainbow Flick is a popular skill and one of the first I ever learned, before I really knew what freestyle football was. It's a very common skill used in football, I remember seeing Maradona doing it and that inspired me to practice it in my garden for hours and hours.

1 You want to start with the football in front of you and, as you approach it, bring one foot over the top of the ball.

2 With your other foot a couple of inches back and to the side, bring that foot to the ball and bring both your feet together with the ball wedged in between.

3 Roll the ball up the back of your front leg with your back foot. Keep your hands out for balance and come up on to the toes of your front foot.

4 Press off from the ground with your front foot and flick your back leg off the ground. heeling (flicking) the ball up.

Players like Neymar and Messi are doing this trick all the time and although it's quite a fancy-looking move, it's very simple to learn.

5 The ball is flicked up behind you and in the air. The idea of this trick is to get the ball as high as you can over your own head. In a football game, if you can get it over an opponent's head as you move forward, the trick is even better!

Reverse Step-over

2.0 RATING ★★★★★ **SKILL LEVEL**

This sounds complicated but once you put all the moves together it flows really easily.

1 Roll the ball back on your strongest foot (I am left-footed, so I always start with that), and roll it back in a straight line.

2 Then as the ball moves back, you step backwards, circling over the ball with your other foot.

3 As the ball continues to roll, you step back across with your stronger foot, so you are making a figure of eight.

You can practise running backwards and moving your feet in a figure of eight sequence without using a ball to begin with. It will help you find a rhythm and get the right movement with your legs. Aim for a mid-pace jogging speed.

4 While you are stepping backwards in time with the ball, it runs in a straight line without you touching it again.

5 You are aiming to move backwards at the same speed as the ball.

6 Try to keep a good rhythm with your legs while you are doing the step-overs.

My Dream Team

I often get asked who my favourite football players are and who would I like to see in a 'dream team'. Here is a list of my top eleven footballers.

Why not make a list of who you want in your squad, too?

Formation

I am going for a 4–3–3 formation …

STRIKERS
9 Cristiano Ronaldo
10 Lionel Messi
11 Ronaldo Lima

All three amazingly skilful strikers – in my mind the best of the best.

LEFT MIDFIELD
6 Ronaldinho

One of the first football players I ever saw performing freestyle football and a big pioneer for the sport. He is amazing at controlling the ball.

CENTRE MIDFIELD
7 Zinedine Zidane

One of my all-time favourite players, he's scored more outrageous goals that anyone I've ever seen. A joy to watch.

LEFT CENTRE-BACK
3 Franz Beckenbauer

A massive legend, he played in three World Cups for West Germany. He is nicknamed 'Der Kaiser' (the Emperor) because of his dominance on the pitch. He was a very stylish player.

RIGHT MIDFIELD
8 Paul Scholes

He played for Manchester United when I was a young supporter and he's played for England. I liked his character: a quiet guy, he worked hard and played well. I could relate to him.

RIGHT CENTRE-BACK
4 Fabio Cannavaro

He captained Italy to win the World Cup in 2006 and is just so solid on the ball. I played foot- volleyball with him on Copacabana Beach during the World Cup in Brazil.

RIGHT BACK
5 Cafu

The most capped Brazilian player of all time, he took part in three World Cup Finals with his national team, winning it twice.

SUBS BENCH
Pelé

Maradona

Oliver Kahn

David Beckham

Bobby Charlton

Paolo Maldini

LEFT BACK
2 Roberto Carlos

One of my favourite players ever and also a good friend. He is amazing in defence but could strike a ball well too. He scored one of the best free kicks I've ever seen, against the French keeper, Fabien Barthez.

GOALKEEPER
1 Peter Schmeichel

I was a big Manchester United fan when I was younger, and he was their goalkeeper. He saved the team so many times. I thought he was the best keeper in the world.

Your Dream Team

Think about what the players bring to the team and why you rate them. List your Dream Team here:

UPFRONT

CENTRE MIDFIELD

LEFT MIDFIELD

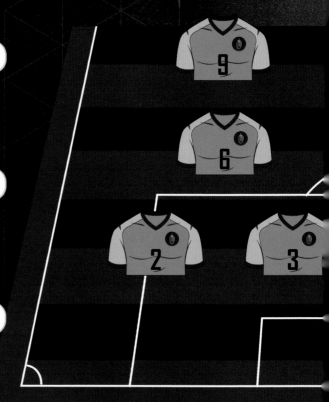

LEFT CENTRE-BACK

LEFT BACK

RIGHT MIDFIELD

> [blank field]

RIGHT CENTRE-BACK

> [blank field]

RIGHT BACK

> [blank field]

SUBS BENCH

> [blank field]

> [blank field]

> [blank field]

GOALKEEPER

> [blank field]

Shoulder Juggles

2.0 RATING ★★☆☆☆ **SKILL LEVEL**

1 Have your feet shoulder-width apart and turn your body inwards so that the shoulder you are practising with is over the centre line of your body.

2 Try to look at the ball as much as you can, staying focused.

3 Start by only shouldering the ball up roughly about 10 inches or so, not too far that you lose control. As your confidence grows you can go higher but control is the key.

4 Aim for the ball to hit your shoulder on the point that the shoulder socket meets the arm, the top point of your shoulder.

Another fundamental move, shoulder juggles are fun to practise and adapt as you become more confident.

Sits Crossover

2.0 RATING ★★★★★

SKILL LEVEL

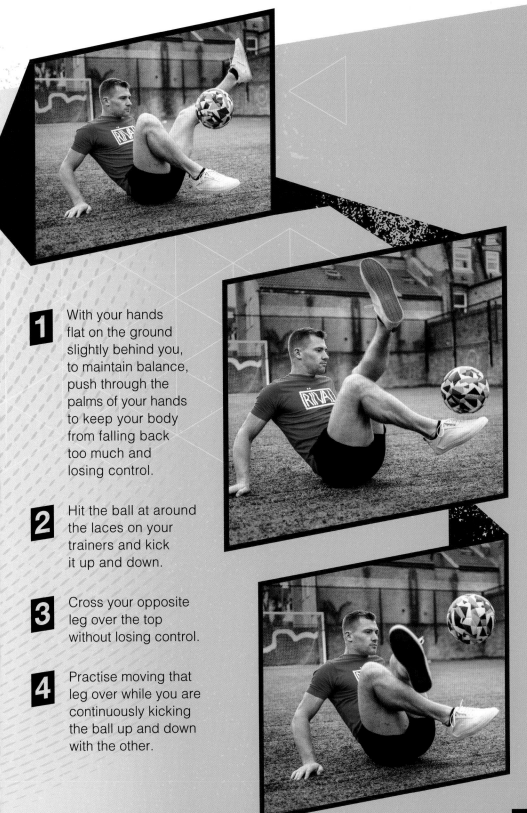

1. With your hands flat on the ground slightly behind you, to maintain balance, push through the palms of your hands to keep your body from falling back too much and losing control.

2. Hit the ball at around the laces on your trainers and kick it up and down.

3. Cross your opposite leg over the top without losing control.

4. Practise moving that leg over while you are continuously kicking the ball up and down with the other.

Sits X-over

2.0 RATING ★★ ☆☆☆

SKILL LEVEL

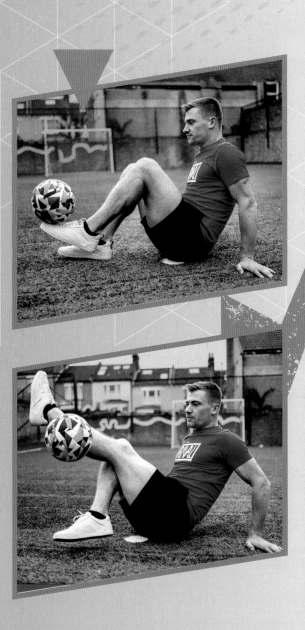

1 This is quite similar to the crossover. Starting in the same body position, you want the ball up in the air around about knee height again, to keep control.

2 Juggle the ball up with your strong foot and then cross your other leg over the one juggling.

3 With your lower leg, you are going to hit the ball again and when the ball goes up in the air, you uncross your feet.

4 And go back into juggles.

Q&A

Heroes

Who is your favourite footballer at the moment?

Currently I'm really impressed by Robert Lewandowski and also Neymar.

What about your all-time favourite footballer?

Can I choose three? They would be David Beckham, Ronaldo Lima and Pelé.

Who are your sporting idols?

Mike Tyson, Muhammad Ali, Georges St-Pierre, Jonah Lomu, Ronaldo Lima and Mr Woo (Woo Hee-young).

Have you ever been starstruck?

The closest I have been to being starstruck was when I met David Beckham in Macau. We were sitting in a room together and watching football on a big projector screen. The footage was of him scoring from a free kick against Greece in 2001. It was a kick that sent England to the World Cup and it was a very surreal moment, being in the same room as Beckham as he watched himself score on the screen. I remember exactly where I was when I saw that match as a youngter, and being with him now, it gave me goosebumps.

Which sports star would you like to teach one freestyle trick to and why?

Conor McGregor, a multiple-weight boxing world champion and Ultimate Fighting Championship (UFC) fighter. He's probably one of the most famous mixed martial artists in the world right now and is a master of movement, so I think he would be able to learn some technical tricks quite quickly. It would be very interesting to spend the day with him and I would probably learn from it, too.

Which sport haven't you tried that you would love to have a go at?

High diving. That would be cool. I can already do some flips and I'm not scared of heights, so it would be perfect.

Which sports do you like watching on TV?

I love watching mixed martial arts (MMA), UFC and any other sort of combat sports. I also like watching rugby, tennis, football, and I love the Olympic Games.

Which one game or sporting event would you watch on repeat?

When Manchester United won the Champions League or when Liverpool beat AC Milan to win the Champions League, coming back from 3–0 down. They would both be fun to watch on repeat.

If you could be a professional sportsman in any other sport, what would it be?

Mixed Martial Arts. I am going to be a professional in MMA, that's my next goal. You've got to have ambition and I spar with professionals every week, so I'm getting there. But it's very tough!

Which sports star would you like to be stuck on a desert island with?

It depends how long I'm there for! Is there any source of food? I have to think carefully in case I have to eat the person I chose! ... I'm joking! I think I would go for Neymar. He'd be cool and he's skilful, so I can help him with some tricks and he can help me with some football techniques. I don't think we would be bored and he's a really funny, happy guy, so we'd have fun.

Sole Juggles

4.0 RATING ★★★★★ **SKILL LEVEL**

The technique to use for sole juggles is to imagine you are riding a bike upside down, that's the sort of movement you need to make with your legs. If you can build up that sort of rhythm, you are going to learn the trick a lot faster.

Sole juggles is one of the most famous freestyle football moves. It's basically about controlling the ball with the soles of your feet while you are lying down.

1 Start by sitting on the floor with your hands flat down by your sides and the ball between your feet in front of you.

2 Now lean back keeping the ball between your legs, with your back on the floor and your head up.

3 Flick the ball up and release it, trying to then catch it and balance it on the sole of your foot.

4 Once you feel you have got a good sense of balance with the ball on your foot, throw the ball onto the foot you want start juggling with.

5 Move your legs into the cycling position and keep the ball juggling in the air, keeping a good rhythm.

Without the ball, practice moving your legs in the cycling position. It will help you get used to moving your legs rhythmically for this skill.

TOP TIP

It will be difficult to balance on your foot straight away, so practice lying down and ask a training partner to place the ball on the sole of your foot while you are on your back. It will really help you get a feel for the ball in the position it is meant to be in.

TOP TIP

You will spend a lot of time getting up and lying back down as the ball drops and rolls off your foot, so I would advise you to practise this in a small room or next to a wall. Otherwise you will be forever wasting time chasing it across an open area. This way you will maximize the amount of training you get done.

Cristiano Ronaldo

"Cristiano is one of the most skilful players in the world and he landed some of the tricks I taught him really quickly."

Cristiano Ronaldo is one of the world's most famous footballers and I got invited over to Madrid, where he was playing at the time, to meet him. My job was to choreograph some skills that he would be performing for an advertisement.

I had to create and plan the concept for the advert and then show him what to do. Of course, he could do a lot of the tricks already, this is one of the most skilful players in the world, but he had to be able to do it in the right way to look good on camera. And I have never worked with someone who was so motivated! He was amazing in that sense. He was focused the whole time on what I was teaching him and what he had to do, and his commitment throughout was impressive. It is very rare to meet someone who is so driven. Even during our breaks from filming, he wanted to learn some new skills, so I showed him some tricks and we played around a bit and I have to say, that was pretty cool.

NEVER JUDGE A BOOK BY ITS COVER

I was inspired by how humble and modest Ronaldo was. He is one of the highest-paid, most famous footballers to have played the game and when you see him on TV and in interviews, 'humble' may not be the first word you think of. But the truth is, he is a deeply passionate sportsman and was incredibly friendly. He has time for everyone. We performed one trick where he had to kick a drone out of the sky with a football. The shot was performed over a small river and the water was freezing cold. Of course, there were lots of times that when he kicked the ball, it would drop into the river. There was a person on set whose only job was to go into the river and get the ball, but sometimes Ronaldo would just jump in and retrieve the ball. He didn't care about getting wet or cold, and he didn't act like he was too famous or too important to jump in the river and get his own ball. He just got involved and got stuck right in.

Around the World

2.0 RATING ★★☆☆☆ **SKILL LEVEL**

(ATW)

A key element of freestyle is to combine different tricks, and Around the World is a very good linking trick when performing a sequence, making it a really important skill to learn.

1 Start by juggling the ball with your strong foot around knee height and then bend your standing leg.

2 Once you are in this position, bring your strong foot from the outside of the ball towards the inside of the ball, lightly touching or skimming it to prepare for bringing your leg around the ball. Put your hands out for balance.

3 Lift your leg up in one fluid motion and start bringing it around the ball.

4 Keep the ball around knee height, bringing your leg and foot up no higher than your hip or chest height.

5 Complete the revolution of the ball, going around it with your foot to get ready to control it back into a neutral juggling position.

This is the world's most popular football trick and it's the one I always get asked to perform for fans.

CERTIFICATE

The most rugby ball neck throw and catches in 30 seconds is 20 and was achieved by Andrew Henderson (UK) on CBBC's Officially Amazing, in London, UK, on 19 October 2016.

OFFICIALLY AMAZING

RECORD HOLDER

CERTIFICATE

The fastest time to complete 10 Maradona sevens, is 37.4 seconds, achieved by Andrew Henderson (UK) on the set of *Blue Peter*, on 16 June 2016

OFFICIALLY AMAZING

RECORD HOLDER

WORLD RECORD BREAKER!

I held the Guinness World Record for the most Around the Worlds in sixty seconds a few years ago – 104! When I beat the record, I beat it by a long way and I was doing around 104 every time in training, so in the build-up to the attempt, I was confident. You have to train very specifically on that one skill, and that requires a lot of dedication. When I performed the World Record attempt in Kuwait it was 40°C and very humid so I think if I ever was going to try to break the current record (set at 106 in 2019), I could give it a good go. Or why not give it a go yourself?

CHALLENGE YOURSELF!

How many Around the Worlds can you do in a row? Once you have mastered doing it one way, try doing it in the other direction. Then use your weak foot and challenge yourself to see how many you can do with that foot. Be consistent, see how many times you can do it out of ten attempts, then beat your record. Next, see how many times you can do it in a row, then see if you can do one, a few juggles and do it again. There are lots of fun challenges you can set yourself with this trick.

Around the Moon

2.5 RATING ★★★☆☆ *SKILL LEVEL*

(ATM)

TOP TIP

This is quite an easy trick to learn but it's hard to perfect the circular motion of your head and keep that movement smooth. Your tricks should be clean and performed with style, so once you have practised it a few times, really focus on making the movement polished.

With this trick, the ball is the moon and your head is in orbit around it. There are lots of variations of this trick used in the freestyle world and when you are competing at a high level, it's a fundamental upper-body skill you'll need to perform. You will have to learn, practise, and perfect this skill if you want to be a good freestyler.

1 Start in the neck stall position (see page 148) and then twist your upper body to one side and use the momentum to move the ball up towards your shoulder.

2 You will need to do a slight shoulder shrug when the ball gets to the end of your shoulder to move the ball.

3 With the ball now released into the air, start to bring your head back around behind it in a circular motion.

4 With your head behind the ball, you are continuing the circular motion.

5 You finish the sequence in the neck stall position, with the ball under control.

Anthony Joshua

> **'** AJ never stops wanting to learn and was constantly asking questions. That is so important. You should never stop being curious. **'**

When I first met AJ he had just fought Andy Ruiz Jr, an American-Mexican boxer whom many people thought wouldn't stand a chance against AJ. But the British boxer was beaten by him and lost his World Championship titles. It was the first time in his professional career that he had suffered such a defeat.

I was invited along to meet him and come up with some ideas for variations in his training routine as he built up to the big rematch with Ruiz. AJ and I were both world champions in our respective fields, and before we started work I really wanted to get to know him a bit better.

I found out that he really loved freestyle football. He kept asking me to show him more and more skills, which was pretty cool! He told me he really liked to dance and he found freestyle football quite similar to both dance and boxing. No, that's not crazy before you say it! Think about your body when you perform freestyle football, and now think about boxing and dance. It's all about movement or, more specifically, rhythm and timing.

ANDREW VS ANTHONY: THE TWO-TOUCH CHAMPIONSHIP!

AJ and I played a game of two-touch, where you have to keep the ball off the ground, using your feet typically, but you can use your knees, shoulders or head. You are only allowed two touches, and the pass to your partner must be made on the second touch. If you drop the ball, don't control it properly or do a bad pass, the other person gets a point. We played first to five points and also wore boxing gloves, which meant we could punch the ball back and forth too, which levelled the playing field a bit. Who won? I did! This is a great game to play with a training partner or a friend. It's all about concentration and control, plus it's loads of fun.

'Rhythm and timing, the basics of freestyle football and boxing.'

AJ set me an interesting challenge when I met him. He asked me to stall a ball on my head while hitting pads that he was holding. I had to maintain a dual focus of keeping the ball balanced on my head while coordinating punches. I think I did quite well. I always like to accept a good challenge when I'm given one!

WHAT IS ADVERSITY? ADVICE FROM A WORLD CHAMPION ...

I asked AJ what adversity meant to him. He was training to fight in a big rematch and I wanted to know how he dealt with that situation. He told me that adversity was like coming over a hurdle that someone had put in front of you. Anxiety is when you put barriers up in front of yourself, but adversity comes from other people. And you need to have the power to get over those hurdles. And not just step over them either – kick or punch them out of the way! You must believe in your own instinct. You are the one who has got yourself here, so you must never forget that.

Never stop wanting to learn

One thing that I discovered when I met Anthony was why he is a champion. I am not talking about the physical effort – of course he works hard, he trains hard, he's very gifted and he's devoted his life to the sport of boxing. But what makes him a champion is that he's always curious and asking questions all the time. He quizzed me on what I thought he could do to improve his boxing.

And I thought to myself, 'Hang on, I don't know anywhere near as much about boxing as you!'

But I think he wanted a different perspective from someone who does another sport. He knew that I sometimes trained six, seven or eight hours a day and what he was asking wasn't about freestyle football but about alternative ways of training and a different mindset. And perhaps, by learning something that someone else does, he might be able to implement it within his boxing training. I thought that was a very honest approach to improving. This is a guy who is earning millions of pounds every fight he does, he's a world champion and very famous, and yet he was asking questions about my training routine!

He has a constant 'learning' approach, and that is so important: never stop wanting to gain knowledge and always feel like you have something to learn. Maybe for Anthony, this mentality only materialized after his big loss and he realized what defeat felt like. He acknowledged that he wasn't invincible. He knew he had a lot of work to do and if he went back into that rematch with the same attitude and mindset as he had had in the first fight, he would probably lose again. But if he came in with a new approach, opened his mind and worked in a new way, it would bring different results. And it did, because he won.

Chest Stall

2.0 RATING ★★ ★ ★ ★
SKILL LEVEL

TOP TIP

It's important to warm up for this trick, as it's not a natural position. It's all about the right balance, so start with steps 1 and 2 and see how long you are comfortable holding the pose. Then you can start working on your balance and practising with a ball.

The best thing to do before you bring a ball into this trick is to get used to the position your body needs to be in to complete the move. This is a good warm-up exercise and will help you understand the position.

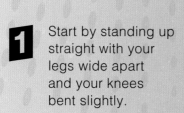 Start by standing up straight with your legs wide apart and your knees bent slightly.

2 Now lean back as far as you can that feels comfortable. You want to maintain balance and stillness. Put your arms up for support and try to hold that for a few seconds before returning to the standing position.

THROWING THE BALL INTO A CHEST STALL

1 Start with the ball in your hands.

2 Gently throw the ball up and back towards you as you move into position. Bend your body just ahead of the movement of the ball.

CHEST STALL WITH THE BALL

1 Hold the ball up in front of you with the top of the ball in line with your chin.

2 Bring the ball back towards your chest as you get into the chest stall position.

3 Hold the ball in between your chin and the top part of your chest, and then slowly release your hands from the ball, fingertip by fingertip, until you are controlling the ball in the chest stall position.

CHEST STALL FROM FOOT JUGGLES

1 Flick the ball up from a foot juggle, slightly back towards you.

2 Bend into the chest stall position, following the movement of the ball and trying to absorb the ball so that it cushions down nicely on your chest and you stall the ball.

How low can you go?!

Crossover

This is a lower-body, popular freestyle move and one I have seen many football players perform. Neymar and Ronaldo use it a lot in training but it's not a skill to try in the game itself.

1 Do a few foot juggles and, when you are ready, kick the ball up higher and bring your strong foot over the top of the ball.

2 At the same time as jumping off the ground with your standing leg, bring that foot up so that your laces connect with the ball and you kick it straight back up.

123

3 Land and control the ball back into foot juggles.

4 Have your arms out wide to keep your body balanced when jumping, and don't put too much power into the kick as you don't want to lose control of the ball.

BREAKING DOWN THE CROSSOVER

1 Start by dropping the ball on the ground and practise bringing your leg over the ball in the crossover movement.

2 When you have that movement well rehearsed, bring in juggles and practice the crossover from juggles before bringing it back under control.

Head Stall

2.0
RATING ★★☆☆☆
SKILL LEVEL

This is a very popular freestyle trick and a lot of freestylers learned it by watching Ronaldinho, a football legend and an early pioneer in the sport of freestyle football. With his Brazilian flair and excitement, he inspired a lot of people (myself included!) to learn this trick.

1 Start with your legs shoulder-width apart, slightly bend your knees and have your head pointed up towards the sky, with your arms out wide for support. This is the basic head stall position.

2 Take the ball and put it up onto your forehead, keeping both hands either side of the ball, and then slowly release, fingertip by fingertip, and see for how long you can balance the ball on your head.

3 The ball will drop off your head, but if you can, try to follow the ball in the direction that it is going. For example, if the ball feels as though it is dropping in front of you, step forwards slightly, if it goes to the right, move to the right, etc. You only want to move very slightly, however, it's very common for people to overreact to the ball's movement and panic, making their body move and jerk all over the place.

Ronaldinho is a former Brazilian professional footballer, considered by some to be the greatest attacking midfield player of his generation because of his creativity, flair and tricks when on the ball. He would warm up on the pitch with a range of freestyle skills and regularly impress the fans with his command of the ball when performing head stalls and other tricks.

4 Stay nice and relaxed and calm, and only make small adjustments so you are keeping the ball under control. This does take a lot of practise as you have to build up some muscle memory, so you will need to be patient when learning this trick. But once you land it, it's a very impressive trick to do. It's definitely worth taking your time and practising over and over again until you get it well controlled and spot on.

Homie Touzani Around the World

4.0
RATING
★★★★★
SKILL LEVEL

(HTATW)

This is an advanced lower body freestyle skill and a combination of two tricks – Around the World and Hop the World – without a touch in between. In freestyle we call this 'no touch', where two separate tricks form one whole new trick.

One of the most famous freestyle footballers, Soufiane Touzani, created an ATW crossover with no touch (see page 168) then this trick was created by a Japanese freestyler called Homie.

TOP TIP

Make sure that you are confident in ATW (see page 102) and HTW (see page 133) first before you try and put the two together. This is a great way to advance those two skills, but you need to have mastered them both independently first.

1 Start by doing an ATW motion, but don't think you have to let the ball go extra high – this is a common mistake. It needs to be a normal height ATW, making sure that you keep nice and relaxed.

2 With your ATW foot at the top of its rotation above the ball, start to jump up with your other foot so that both feet are up in the air, your second foot ready to rotate.

3 Bring your second leg round the ball with an inside rotation, landing and bringing the ball under control with foot juggles to finish.

HTATW is one of the hardest tricks you can do. There is a funny video of Neymar trying to do it, when he lands on top of the ball and falls over – so don't be frustrated if you fail. Take your time and work through the basics – but keep going!

Hop the World

2.0 RATING

★★★★★ *SKILL LEVEL*

(HTW)

This is one of the most performed freestyle tricks in the world. It's used by a lot of freestylers and football players. It is an essential move for doing combinations in freestyle and is one of the first freestyle tricks I ever learned. It's a beginner's trick but you will need to focus and practise.

1 Start by doing juggles to get the ball off the ground and then, with your strong foot, kick the ball straight up to knee height.

2 Then, with a little hop, take your leg over the ball.

3 Bring your leg round quickly and smoothly, and control the ball with your strong foot.

4 And at the end, go back into juggles. When you are up in the air, make sure you keep your hands out for balance. Practise with both feet.

Lemmens Around the World

4.0 RATING
★★★★☆
SKILL LEVEL

(LATW)

This trick was created by a freestyler called Martin Lemmens, who was the first person ever to do a double Around the World without a touch in between the two tricks.

Basically, you kick the ball up with your strong foot, bringing your leg around the ball twice, in the same direction, and then you touch it again with your strong foot to complete the trick.

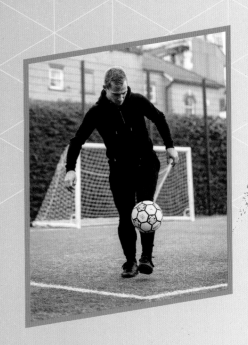

1 Start with the ball juggling on your strong foot.

2 Once you have started the motion for the first ATW, stay nice and relaxed, and bring your leg up slightly higher than normal with your toes pointed up. You need to make sure your standing leg is on the floor and ready to go up onto your toes as you move towards the second revolution.

3 Just as you start the second revolution, lift your other foot off the ground in a jump to give yourself enough room to bring your rotating leg around it a second time.

TOP TIP

This isn't about speed. Once you have your ATW consistent, it's all about staying relaxed on the first rotation, but bringing the ball a little higher and timing your jump so that you can do the second rotation while you're up in the air, with enough time to go around it.

4 As you are going around the second revolution of the ball, your standing foot will be going towards the ground and you should be three-quarters of the way through the trick when it lands.

5 Finally, you should make contact with the ball – your standing foot is back on the ground and the foot that has been doing the revolutions around the ball is now underneath the ball. Keep relaxed and in control of the ball as you go back into normal juggles.

Building Your Confidence

> **' Essentially, it was the worst moment of my life, but it has given me the best moments in my life. Remembering that will always give me confidence. '**

When things go wrong

When I was injured, being told I couldn't do sport was probably the worst thing anyone could have ever said to me. It was impossible not to get upset because being active and doing all kinds of sports was who I was. As a kid I was always trying new things and never sitting still, and yet my injury wiped out a whole load of choices for me. Suddenly, I couldn't play anything.

Looking back at that time, it would have been easy to give up and become incredibly angry and frustrated. Sport was everything I ever loved, and I had been told it would be a long time before I could go back to any sort of activity. And even when I recovered, I would have to seriously consider if I wanted to take part in contact sports again. This was the end of my rugby career.

'But when you are faced with something that is out of your control, it is up to you to take back control. '

I was sitting in the hospital bed with my leg in a cast and I was bored. It was quite a depressing time. But my injury didn't define who I was and so even though I couldn't get out of bed, I started balancing a ball on my head. I practised that one move, something I had watched a few football players on TV doing, and then I wanted to learn more and more and more ...

What has freestyle football taught me?

The way that freestyle has helped me with my confidence is immeasurable. I was a very shy kid at school, and if I was asked a question in class, I would go bright red. I was always too shy to speak, even though I knew the answer. Freestyle boosted my confidence, to the point where I can now perform in front of 85,000 people in a half-time show at Old Trafford, at a World Championship final or in front of one of the best football players in the world and not be anxious at all. I can control my nerves and perform to the best of my ability each time.

With freestyle, when you learn a skill, you practise and practise until you land it. And then you move on to the next skill because you have mastered one and are now ready for the next, which boosts your confidence. And then, when people say what you're doing is cool and comment on your skills, it reinforces that you can do it. You are the one who has put in the time to learn, you are the one who has mastered a skill and that should give you a lot of confidence.

'Learning new skills gave me a lot of confidence and as your confidence grows you look for new challenges. I am always seeking new challenges, probably because overcoming the adversity of the injury made me more determined. '

Neck Stall

1.0 RATING

SKILL LEVEL

This is a freestyle football upper-body skill where you balance the ball on your neck, in the groove between the base of your head and your back. It's one of the first skills that every freestyler needs to learn, it was probably the second freestyle football trick I ever learned.

1 Start with your legs slightly wider than shoulder-width apart and your toes pointed slightly outwards, with your feet flat on the ground.

2 With the ball in your hands, bring your arms over your head and rest it in the groove while keeping the ball still in your hands.

3 Now bend your knees and start looking forwards, making your back as flat as it can be. Begin to release the ball, fingertip by fingertip.

4 As you move your hands away from the ball, bring your arms out to the side for additional support. Remember to keep your head up and looking forwards. Aim to hold this position for around five seconds or longer.

149

TOP TIP

Start by learning the
position you need to be
in for this trick before you
bring in the ball. It will help
you feel more confident
landing the skill if you
have perfected this
unusual stance.

Neck Stall Push-up

3.0 RATING ★★★★★ *SKILL LEVEL*

The neck stall push-up is fairly self-explanatory – we are essentially doing a neck stall and a push-up! Practise your push-ups first to get a slow and steady rhythm going before you introduce the ball.

1 Start off in the neck stall position and then slowly go down onto one knee. Don't move quickly, keep yourself nice and steady.

2 Put your other knee on the floor now, still moving slowly, so the ball is steady on your neck, and then bring your hands to the ground one at a time.

3 Slowly extend one of your legs right back behind you, so the toes of that foot are on the floor and your body is nice and straight. Make sure your head is up and looking forwards.

4 Fully extend your other leg behind you and aim to balance the ball for at least five seconds in this position before attempting to do any push-ups.

5 Start your first push-up when you are ready, keeping your head forwards and your body nice and straight. Do it slowly so the ball doesn't move. If you are finding full push-ups hard, practise doing them on your knees first.

CHALLENGE TIME!

See how many push-ups you can do without dropping the ball! Set yourself a target number or count how many you can manage in a minute.

Neck Stall Handstand

5.0 RATING ★★★★★ *SKILL LEVEL*

This is one of the toughest skills to perform. You need to have mastered the neck stall and be able to do a strong handstand as well. Keep working on the neck stall until you feel confident about moving on to this one. It's always better to land a trick securely and repeatedly before you advance it.

1 Begin in the neck stall position and then start to crouch down, making sure your hands are ready to move towards the floor.

2 Now you have rested your hands on the floor, you might need to stand on your toes slightly to keep a good balance.

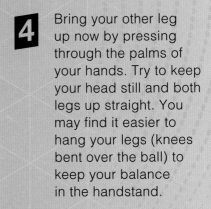

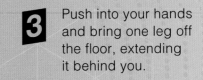

3 Push into your hands and bring one leg off the floor, extending it behind you.

4 Bring your other leg up now by pressing through the palms of your hands. Try to keep your head still and both legs up straight. You may find it easier to hang your legs (knees bent over the ball) to keep your balance in the handstand.

TOP TIP

Practise your handstand against a wall for support and to get used to the position. When you are ready to move away from the wall, make sure there are no other obstacles around and you have plenty of space to practise. You will need to stretch and warm up properly before you begin, and don't worry if you can't hold the handstand for that long at first. The better you are at the handstand, the better you will be at this trick.

Q&A
Skills, Secrets & Future Goals

Which skill do you enjoy performing the most?

Backflip moves always impress the crowds, but my favourite has to be the Triple Around the World.

What skill took you the longest to learn?

Triple Around the World. I have actually completed four revolutions a few times, but I haven't filmed it. I know people believe that I have done it, but it doesn't count in this sport unless it's recorded. To do four revolutions with one foot is as far as the body can go. No one would ever do five.

What was the first skill you learned to perform?

Thigh catch – catching the ball between the calf and the hamstring.

What is your biggest fear?

Having regrets about the things I didn't do. When I was eighteen years old, I had the choice of going to university or competing in the World Championships to fulfil my dream. Everyone was telling me to go to uni, but I knew what I wanted to do and that if I didn't take that chance to be a champion right now, I might never get it again. But I *would* be able to go to university at another point in my life if I chose to. It was the best decision I ever made. I think if I had gone to uni I would have had a lot of regrets.

How many footballs do you own?

I used to own hundreds, but I have given a lot away over the years on photo shoots and as part of training camps and to fans, so now I think I have around fifty or sixty. Still quite a lot!

Where do you see yourself in ten years' time?

I hope to have my own academy for freestyle football and a black belt in martial arts! I will still be living in England and hopefully have some kids of my own.

What is the best thing about being a freestyle football world champion?

The fact that I can travel around the world and inspire people of all ages and from different cultural backgrounds. Being a positive role model is very rewarding. I love learning and teaching new skills, and seeing people enjoying freestyle and keeping themselves healthy.

Who has been the biggest influence on your career?

My father. He's always told me that I shouldn't ever give up and should always try. He assured me I can do things – if I told him I wanted to play football when I was younger, he'd say, 'OK, go on then, try your best!' He would never knock my confidence and would always remind me to keep pushing for my dreams. He never allowed me to let any negative experiences define me. He was very inspiring and I want to do him proud.

One thing I always do before competing is to go away from everyone else and find a quiet corner of a room. Even if it is in a busy place with lots of people, I will take myself off and stare at a wall, just focusing on the task at hand. I concentrate on breathing, for a good five to ten minutes, and it helps me to prepare. Sometimes, in the weeks before a big competition, I will stop training and take some time out. It helps me to have a good understanding of what I need to do. I visualize what I am going to do in order to win. The more I think about it, the clearer the visions become. Working on that mental focus, with no distractions, is very important.

Tell us something we don't know about you ...

I have hundreds of scars on my body, more than 200, from loads of different things: rugby, lots of little bumps and scrapes and cuts from jumping off things and getting stitches. But I'm not embarrassed by them, they are part of me. You shouldn't let anything like that knock your confidence, as they make you who you are, all these war wounds. And I am still getting scars – even now!

Side Head Stall

The side head stall is one of my favourite freestyle football tricks and it's one of the skills I am most known for doing! I have created a lot of variations from this skill too – I can balance the ball on the side of my head in a handstand and I can do multiple revolutions of the ball with my legs by flicking it up from this side head stall position.

2 Now go into the side head stall position without the ball by leaning over to one side as if you are stretching the side of your body. Bring your arm over the top and then your other arm down in a straight line, keeping your head flat so you can balance the imaginary ball there.

1 Start with your legs shoulder-width apart, toes slightly pointed outwards and your knees slightly bent, so you aren't too stiff.

3 Next, you are going to get into that position and add in the football.

4 Slowly let go of the ball, fingertip by fingertip. See how long you can balance it for. Position it just in front of your ear, so it rests on the side of your head, just touching your ear.

5 Hold that position for as long as you can, between three and five seconds, before you progress to the next step, which is to catch the ball into a side head stall after throwing it in.

SIDE HEAD STALL
FROM THROW IN

1 Start with the ball in your hands, and throw it up in front of you, but slightly to one side.

2 Always make sure you are looking at the ball, following the motion of the ball.

3 Cushion the ball as it comes down, getting into that side head stall position.

Carousel

3.0 RATING ★★★☆ **SKILL LEVEL**

This seems like such a hard trick, but it's really not, it just looks super impressive! It's a move that was originally created in freestyle basketball but it's a big freestyle football trick and one that gets a huge reaction when you perform it in competitions.

1 Start with the ball pressed up against your forehead with your palms facing out. Your arms should form a diamond shape.

2 Roll the ball down onto one of your arms. If you drop the ball to your left, you turn to your right. If you drop the ball to your right, you turn to your left. I am dropping the ball to my left arm, and moving to my right.

3 Keep your hands and your upper-body in the same position the whole way through, as you are moving the ball by bending your back and your knees as you turn around.

4 Keep turning in a circular motion until you get to a neck stall position, but you don't want the ball to stall, you are just using it as a path for your next position. Keep turning around on the same spot, maintaining a smooth, consistent pace the whole way through.

TOP TIP

You might get dizzy when practising this so take lots of breaks!

5 Roll the ball onto your right arm from your shoulder and keep turning.

6 Repeat the process, trying to keep the ball flowing in one path. Imagine the ball is on a rollercoaster ride between your hands and your head and you have to keep the ball and your body moving at the same speed. If you twist too fast, you will drop the ball, and if you go too slow it won't be fluid. Once you have completed the turn once, keep going and see how many you can do.

Top Head Stall

1.0 RATING ★☆☆☆☆ *SKILL LEVEL*

This is one of my signature freestyle moves and I love how much fun you can have with it, you can really test your skills. I can walk around, sit down, climb ladders ... I can even ride a bike with the ball on my head.

1 Start with your legs shoulder-width apart and then place the ball above your head before setting it down on the 'groove' at the top of your head. This might not be in the centre of your head as the groove spot can be different for everyone.

2 Once you have found that spot, slowly release the ball, fingertip by fingertip.

3 Keep your hands out for balance as they move away from the ball, and stay as still as possible: any slight movement will result in the ball moving and it will be very difficult to control. If the ball starts to move, follow the direction of it – nice and slowly – try not to jerk or move too quickly.

CHALLENGE!

Count how many seconds you are holding the ball for each time you try and then aim to beat your record. Use your legs and upper body to move if the ball starts to fall because you need to keep your neck and your head still and always facing forward in the same position. It will feel awkward at first, but after a while it will be second nature.

I have boxed with Anthony Joshua while balancing a ball on my head and I have even climbed the Great Wall of China with a ball on my head! It was one of the riskiest freestyle stunts I have ever completed and yes, I did manage to make it to the top before you ask. I think I am the only person ever to have done that – I do like a challenge!

TOP TIP

Practise this skill in front of a mirror so you can see where the ball is going, what position to be in, and how to adapt and adjust to keep it balanced on top of your head. If you can draw a small spot on the mirror that will really help you focus on one spot. It will feel strange but even if the ball moves, try to keep you head in the same position so you get used to keeping your head and shoulders still. You need to keep repeating this, it does take time and I would recommend practising at least ten minutes a day to begin with. You will get there eventually!

Touzani Around the World

3.0 RATING

★★★★☆ **SKILL LEVEL**

(TATW)

This is a combination of two lower-body freestyle tricks, the first is the ATW and the second is a crossover. Make sure you are confident in those separate skills as you will be combining both together in one fluid movement.

Soufiane Touzani created this trick so it's named after him, and I have been lucky enough to meet and train with him. He told me I was his favourite freestyler and that was crazy because he was the reason I got into freestyle football. He is an idol of mine.

1 Begin by doing foot juggles with the ball, around about knee height, to get into position for the start of the ATW motion. Start your ATW nice and low. You don't want it higher than knee height.

2 When you are three-quarters of the way ATW, press off from the ground with your opposite foot to jump in the air for the crossover motion.

3 Have your crossover foot up in the air, as your ATW foot makes a connection with the ball and kicks it upwards.

4 Keep your toes pointing upwards, kicking the ball with the bottom of your laces and completing the crossover movement and then controlling the ball back into juggles at the end.

Sofiane Touzani's freestyle videos blew my mind, I thought a lot of the tricks he performed were fake because they looked impossible! I remember watching the videos to try to find the strings he must be using – I didn't think anyone could do with a football what he was doing. Yet now, when I see those videos, they look quite basic compared to what I do today. And that should give you a lot of confidence. Maybe one day you will look back at what I am teaching you and think, that's so basic! Look what I can do now!

Crossbar Challenge

Be creative! Come up with your own crossbar contests or mix up the skills you have learned and create your own challenges. The possibilities are endless.

Hitting the crossbar is a fun and impressive way to finish off a set of skills or simply a good way to improve your target practice. The end result of this trick shot is the same – to hit the crossbar – but I have made the challenges more difficult as you progress with your skills. Good luck!

2.0 RATING ★★☆☆☆ *SKILL LEVEL*

1 Put the ball on the penalty spot then give yourself a short run-up and lean back slightly before you strike the ball.

2 You want to hit the crossbar but it will help if you aim for a smaller target, so I want you to picture a little dot on the bar. Before you kick the ball, focus on that small dot.

3 With practice, even if you miss your spot, you will still hit the crossbar. Whenever you are kicking the ball towards a target, if you make your target size as small as possible, you have more chance of hitting the general area.

3.0 RATING

★★★☆☆

SKILL LEVEL

Once you have practised this from the penalty spot, move the trick up a gear by doing it from juggles.

1 Move back slightly from the goal, but still stay straight in front of it and practise your juggles before volleying the ball. Keep the same idea of aiming at and hitting a small target on the crossbar.

To take it to the next level, we are going to do the same thing but add a skill into the mix before juggles. A good one to do would be a crossover, then juggles, then a volley and then hit the crossbar.

1 As you get more confident with the crossover motion and you have hit the crossbar a couple of times, start performing the trick without the juggles in between. You are now doing a crossover, straight into a volley, and aiming at and hitting the crossbar.

2 Now take it a step even further! Create an angle so you aren't standing directly in front of the goal and move to just outside the penalty box. As you're further away from the target, you will have to adjust the power with which you strike the ball.

I am now challenging you to make it more difficult by hitting the crossbar from sit-down juggles!

This is the ultimate trick shot and one that you should find lots of fun to practise – which is what it's all about.

SKILL LEVEL

★ ★ ★ ★ ★

5.0
RATING

1 With the ball outside of the penalty box, at an angle, I want you to do a no-look crossbar challenge.

2 Sit down, facing away from the goal and volley the ball to the crossbar. Think about the power you need to hit the ball, the movement of your body when you connect with the ball and your target. I KNOW you will be able to do it!

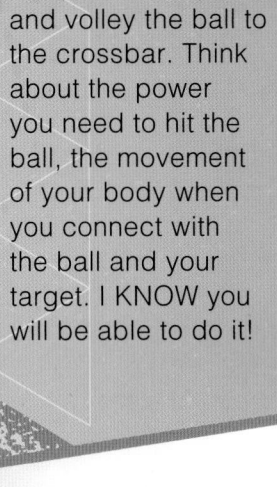

Acknowledgements

This book has been a labour of love. Conceived and produced during a very tough time for us all, the whole team has worked with great resolve and purpose to make this the best introduction to football freestyling.

I would like to thank the following photographers whose fantastic work you see on these pages: Martin Sarga, Scott Penders, Roman Brezovsky and Jordan Mckellar. Thanks to the team at Hire a Pitch in London, especially Jordan, who was so helpful to us when we were shooting. Big thanks to Billingshurst Football Club for letting us use their pitch and to all the children who took part in a training session with me on a rainy Saturday – now you've got no excuse to get those skills working, guys!

Index

First published in Great Britain in 2021 by
Michael O'Mara Books Limited
9 Lion Yard
Tremadoc Road
London SW4 7NQ

A CIP catalogue record for this book is available from the British Library.

ISBN: 978-1-78929-325-8 in paperback print format
ISBN: 978-1-78929-328-9 in e-book format

Designed by Natasha Le Coultre
Front cover photograph by Scott Penders;
Back cover photograph by Martin Sarga
Printed and bound in China by Leo Paper Products

Follow us on Twitter @OMaraBooks

www.mombooks.com

FSC
www.fsc.org

MIX
Paper from
responsible sources
FSC® C020056